JOB

∾

The Message is *a clear
and contemporary paraphrase
of the Bible from the original languages.
The goal of* The Message *is to convert the tone,
rhythm, events, and ideas into the way
we actually think and speak today.*

∾

Other editions of *The Message:*
   The New Testament with Psalms and Proverbs
   The New Testament
   Psalms
   Proverbs
   The Wisdom Books

The MESSAGE

JOB

Led by Suffering
to the Heart of God

Eugene H. Peterson

NAVPRESS

BRINGING TRUTH TO LIFE
NavPress Publishing Group
P.O. Box 35001, Colorado Springs, Colorado 80935

Old Testament Exegetical Consultant:
   Dr. Robert L. Alden
   Denver Seminary

Stylistic Consultant:
   Luci Shaw
   senior editor, Shaw Publishers; writer-in-residence, Regent College

Library of Congress Catalog Card Number:
   95-72091
ISBN 08910-99271

Cover illustration: Steve Eames

Printed in the United States of America

2 3 4 5 6 7 8 9 10 11 12 13 14 15 / 00 99 98 97 96

_____

Published in association with the literary agency of Alive Communications, Inc., 1465 Kelly Johnson Blvd., Suite 320, Colorado Springs, CO 80920.

_____

INTRODUCTION

*J*ob suffered. His name is synonymous with suffering. He asked,
"Why?" He asked, "Why *me*?" And he put his questions to
God. He asked his questions persistently, passionately, and elo-
quently. He refused to take silence for an answer. He refused to take
clichés for an answer. He refused to let God off the hook.

Job did not take his sufferings quietly or piously. He disdained
going for a second opinion to outside physicians or philosophers.
Job took his stance before *God*, and there he protested his suffering,
protested mightily.

It is not only because Job suffered that he is important to us. It is
because he suffered in the same ways that *we* suffer—in the vital
areas of family, personal health, and material things. Job is also important to us because he searchingly questioned and boldly protested his
suffering. Indeed, he went "to the top" with his questions.

It is not suffering as such that troubles us. It is undeserved suffering.

Almost all of us in our years of growing up have the experience of
disobeying our parents and getting punished for it. When that discipline was connected with wrongdoing, it had a certain sense of justice
to it: *When we do wrong, we get punished.*

One of the surprises as we get older, however, is that we come to
see that there is no real correlation between the amount of wrong we
commit and the amount of pain we experience. An even larger sur-
prise is that very often there is something quite the opposite: We do

5

right and get knocked down. We do the best we are capable of doing, and just as we are reaching out to receive our reward we are hit from the blind side and sent reeling.

This is the suffering that first bewilders and then outrages us. This is the kind of suffering that bewildered and outraged Job, for Job was doing everything right when suddenly everything went wrong. And it is this kind of suffering to which Job gives voice when he protests to God.

Job gives voice to his sufferings so well, so accurately and honestly, that anyone who has ever suffered—which includes every last one of us—can recognize his or her personal pain in the voice of Job. Job says boldly what some of us are too timid to say. He makes poetry out of what in many of us is only a tangle of confused whimpers. He shouts out to God what a lot of us mutter behind our sleeves. He refuses to accept the role of a defeated victim.

It is also important to note what Job does *not* do, lest we expect something from him that he does not intend. Job does not curse God as his wife suggests he should do, getting rid of the problem by getting rid of God. But neither does Job *explain* suffering. He does not instruct us in how to live so that we can avoid suffering. Suffering is a mystery, and Job comes to respect the mystery.

In the course of facing, questioning, and respecting suffering, Job finds himself in an even larger mystery—the mystery of God. Perhaps the greatest mystery in suffering is how it can bring a person into the presence of God in a state of worship, full of wonder, love, and praise. Suffering does not inevitably do that, but it does it far more often than we would expect. It certainly did that for Job. Even in his answer to his wife he speaks the language of an uncharted irony, a dark and difficult kind of truth: "We take the good days from God—why not also the bad days?"

But there is more to the book of Job than Job. There are Job's friends. The moment we find ourselves in trouble of any kind—sick in the hospital, bereaved by a friend's death, dismissed from a job or relationship, depressed or bewildered—people start showing up telling us exactly what is wrong with us and what we must do to get better. Sufferers attract fixers the way road-kills attract vultures. At first we are impressed that they bother with us and amazed at their facility with answers. They know so much! How did they get to be such experts in living?

More often than not, these people use the Word of God frequently and loosely. They are full of spiritual diagnosis and prescription. It all sounds so hopeful. But then we begin to wonder, "Why is it that for all their apparent compassion we feel worse instead of better after they've said their piece?"

The book of Job is not only a witness to the dignity of suffering and God's presence in our suffering but is also our primary biblical protest against religion that has been reduced to explanations or "answers." Many of the answers that Job's so-called friends give him are technically true. But it is the "technical" part that ruins them. They are answers without personal relationship, intellect without intimacy. The answers are slapped onto Job's ravaged life like labels on a specimen bottle. Job rages against this secularized wisdom that has lost touch with the living realities of God.

In every generation there are men and women who pretend to be able to instruct us in a way of life that guarantees that we will be "healthy, wealthy, and wise." According to the propaganda of these people, anyone who lives intelligently and morally is exempt from suffering. From their point of view, it is lucky for us that they are now at hand to provide the intelligent and moral answers we need.

On behalf of all of us who have been misled by the platitudes of the nice people who show up to tell us everything is going to be just all right if we simply think such-and-such and do such-and-such, Job issues an anguished rejoinder. He rejects the kind of advice and teaching that has God all figured out, that provides glib explanations for every circumstance. Job's honest defiance continues to be the best defense against the clichés of positive thinkers and the prattle of religious small talk.

The honest, innocent Job is placed in a setting of immense suffering and then surrounded by the conventional religious wisdom of the day in the form of speeches by Eliphaz, Bildad, Zophar, and Elihu. The contrast is unforgettable. The counselors methodically and pedantically recite their bookish precepts to Job. At first Job rages in pain and roars out his protests, but then he becomes silent in awestruck faith before God, who speaks from out of a storm—a "whirlwind" of Deity. Real faith cannot be reduced to spiritual bromides and merchandised in success stories. It is refined in the fires and the storms of pain.

The book of Job does not reject answers as such. There *is* content to biblical religion. It is the *secularization* of answers that is rejected—answers severed from their Source, the living God, the Word that both batters us and heals us. We cannot have truth *about* God divorced from the mind and heart *of* God.

In our compassion, we don't like to see people suffer. And so our instincts are aimed at preventing and alleviating suffering. No doubt that is a good impulse. But if we really want to reach out to others who are suffering, we should be careful not to be like Job's friends, not to do our "helping" with the presumption that we can fix things, get rid of them, or make them "better." We may look at our suffering friends and imagine how they could have better marriages, better behaved children, better mental and emotional health. But when we rush in to fix suffering, we need to keep in mind several things.

First, no matter how insightful we may be, we don't *really* understand the full nature of our friends' problems. Second, our friends may not *want* our advice. Third, the ironic fact of the matter is that more often than not, people do not suffer *less* when they are committed to following God, but *more*. When these people go through suffering, their lives are often transformed, deepened, marked with beauty and holiness, in remarkable ways that could never have been anticipated before the suffering.

So, instead of continuing to focus on preventing suffering—which we simply won't be very successful at anyway—perhaps we should begin *entering* the suffering, participating insofar as we are able—entering the mystery and looking around for God. In other words, we need to quit feeling sorry for people who suffer and instead look up to them, learn from them, and—if they will let us—join them in protest and prayer. Pity can be nearsighted and condescending; shared suffering can be dignifying and life-changing. As we look at Job's suffering and praying and worshiping, we see that he has already blazed a trail of courage and integrity for us to follow.

⌒

But sometimes it's hard to know just how to follow Job's lead when we feel so alone in our suffering, unsure of what God wants us to do. What we must realize during those times of darkness is that the God who appeared to Job in the whirlwind is calling out to all of us. Although God may not appear to us in a vision, he makes himself known to us in all the many ways that he describes to Job—from the macro to the micro, from the wonders of the galaxies to the little things we take for granted. He is the Creator of the unfathomable universe all around us—and he is also the Creator of the universe inside of us. And so we gain hope—not from the darkness of our suffering, not from pat answers in books, but from the God who sees our suffering and shares our pain.

Reading Job prayerfully and meditatively leads us to face the questions that

9

arise when our lives don't turn out the way we expect them to. First we hear all the stock answers. Then we ask the questions again, with variations—and hear the answers again, with variations. Over and over and over. Every time we let Job give voice to our own questions, our suffering gains in dignity and we are brought a step closer to the threshold of the voice and mystery of God. Every time we persist with Job in rejecting the quick-fix counsel of people who see us and hear us but do not understand us, we deepen our availability and openness to the revelation that comes only out of the tempest. The mystery of God eclipses the darkness and the struggle. We realize that suffering calls *our* lives into question, not God's. The tables are turned: God-Alive is present to us. God is speaking to us. And so Job's experience is confirmed and repeated once again in our suffering and our vulnerable humanity.

Job

1

A MAN DEVOTED TO GOD

Job was a man who lived in Uz. He was honest inside and out, a man of his word, who was totally devoted to God and hated evil with a passion. He had seven sons and three daughters. He was also very wealthy—seven thousand head of sheep, three thousand camels, five hundred teams of oxen, five hundred donkeys, and a huge staff of servants—the most influential man in all the East!

His sons used to take turns hosting parties in their homes, always inviting their three sisters to join them in their merry-making. When the parties were over, Job would get up early in the morning and sacrifice a burnt offering for each of his children, thinking, "Maybe one of them sinned by defying God inwardly." Job made a habit of this sacrificial atonement, just in case they'd sinned.

THE FIRST TEST: FAMILY AND FORTUNE

One day when the angels came to report to GOD, Satan, who was the Designated Accuser, came along with them. GOD singled out Satan and said, "What have you been up to?"

Satan answered GOD, "Going here and there, checking things out on earth."

GOD said to Satan, "Have you noticed my friend Job? There's no one quite like him—honest and true to his word, totally devoted to God and hating evil."

Satan retorted, "So do you think Job does all that out of the sheer goodness of his heart? Why, no one ever had it so good!

You pamper him like a pet, make sure nothing bad ever happens to him or his family or his possessions, bless everything he does— he can't lose!

"But what do you think would happen if you reached down and took away everything that is his? He'd curse you right to your face, that's what."

GOD replied, "We'll see. Go ahead—do what you want with all that is his. Just don't hurt *him*." Then Satan left the presence of GOD.

Sometime later, while Job's children were having one of their parties at the home of the oldest son, a messenger came to Job and said, "The oxen were plowing and the donkeys grazing in the field next to us when Sabeans attacked. They stole the animals and killed the field hands. I'm the only one to get out alive and tell you what happened."

While he was still talking, another messenger arrived and said, "Bolts of lightning struck the sheep and the shepherds and fried them—burned them to a crisp. I'm the only one to get out alive and tell you what happened."

While he was still talking, another messenger arrived and said, "Chaldeans coming from three directions raided the camels and massacred the camel drivers. I'm the only one to get out alive and tell you what happened."

While he was still talking, another messenger arrived and said, "Your children were having a party at the home of the oldest brother when a tornado swept in off the desert and struck the house. It collapsed on the young people and they died. I'm the only one to get out alive and tell you what happened."

Job got to his feet, ripped his robe, shaved his head, then fell to the ground and worshiped:

"Naked I came from my mother's womb,
    naked I'll return to the womb of the earth.
GOD gives, GOD takes.
    GOD's name be ever blessed."

Not once through all this did Job sin; not once did he blame God.

2

THE SECOND TEST: HEALTH

One day when the angels came to report to GOD, Satan also showed up. GOD singled out Satan, saying, "And what have you been up to?"

Satan answered GOD, "Oh, going here and there, checking things out."

Then GOD said to Satan, "Have you noticed my friend Job? There's no one quite like him, is there—honest and true to his word, totally devoted to God and hating evil? He still has a firm grip on his integrity! You tried to trick me into destroying him, but it didn't work."

Satan answered, "A human would do anything to save his life. But what do you think would happen if you reached down and took away his health? He'd curse you to your face, that's what."

GOD said, "All right. Go ahead—you can do what you like with him. But mind you, don't kill him."

Satan left GOD and struck Job with terrible sores. Job was ulcers and scabs from head to foot. They itched and oozed so badly that he took a piece of broken pottery to scrape himself, then went and sat on a trash heap, among the ashes.

His wife said, "Still holding on to your precious integrity, are you? Curse God and be done with it!"

He told her, "You're talking like an empty-headed fool. We take the good days from God—why not also the bad days?"

Not once through all this did Job sin. He said nothing against God.

JOB'S THREE FRIENDS

Three of Job's friends heard of all the trouble that had fallen on him. Each traveled from his own country—Eliphaz from Teman, Bildad from Shuah, Zophar from Naamath—and went together to Job to keep him company and comfort him. When they first caught sight of him, they couldn't believe what they saw—they hardly recognized him! They cried out in lament, ripped their robes, and dumped dirt on their heads as a sign of their grief. Then they sat with him on the ground. Seven days and nights they sat there without saying a word. They could see how rotten he felt, how deeply he was suffering.

3   JOB CRIES OUT

WHAT'S THE POINT OF LIFE?

Then Job broke the silence. He spoke up and cursed his fate:

"Obliterate the day I was born.
    Blank out the night I was conceived!
Let it be a black hole in space.

16

May God above forget it ever happened.
Erase it from the books!
May the day of my birth be buried in deep darkness,
    shrouded by the fog,
    swallowed by the night.
And the night of my conception—the devil take it!
    Rip the date off the calendar,
    delete it from the almanac.
Oh, turn that night into pure nothingness—
    no sounds of pleasure from that night, ever!
May those who are good at cursing curse that day.
    Unleash the sea beast, Leviathan, on it.
May its morning stars turn to black cinders,
    waiting for a daylight that never comes,
    never once seeing the first light of dawn.
And why? Because it released me from my mother's womb
    into a life with so much trouble.

"Why didn't I die at birth,
    my first breath out of the womb my last?
Why were there arms to rock me,
    and breasts for me to drink from?
I could be resting in peace right now,
    asleep forever, feeling no pain,
In the company of kings and statesmen
    in their royal ruins,
Or with princes resplendent
    in their gold and silver tombs.
Why wasn't I stillborn and buried
    with all the babies who never saw light,

17

Where the wicked no longer trouble anyone
    and bone-weary people get a long-deserved rest?
Prisoners sleep undisturbed,
    never again to wake up to the bark of the guards.
The small and the great are equals in that place,
    and slaves are free from their masters.

"Why does God bother giving light to the miserable,
    why bother keeping bitter people alive,
Those who want in the worst way to die, and can't,
    who can't imagine anything better than death,
Who count the day of their death and burial
    the happiest day of their life?
What's the point of life when it doesn't make sense,
    when God blocks all the roads to meaning?

"Instead of bread I get groans for my supper,
    then leave the table and vomit my anguish.
The worst of my fears has come true,
    what I've dreaded most has happened.
My repose is shattered, my peace destroyed.
    No rest for me, ever—death has invaded life."

4   ELIPHAZ SPEAKS OUT

NOW *YOU'RE* THE ONE IN TROUBLE

Then Eliphaz from Teman spoke up:

"Would you mind if I said something to you?
    Under the circumstances it's hard to keep quiet.

You yourself have done this plenty of times, spoken words
   that clarify, encouraged those who were about to quit.
Your words have put stumbling people on their feet,
   put fresh hope in people about to collapse.
But now *you're* the one in trouble—you're hurting!
   You've been hit hard and you're reeling from the blow.
But shouldn't your devout life give you confidence now?
   Shouldn't your exemplary life give you hope?

"Think! Has a truly innocent person ever ended up on the
      scrap heap?
   Do genuinely upright people ever lose out in the end?
It's my observation that those who plow evil
   and sow trouble reap evil and trouble.
One breath from God and they fall apart,
   one blast of his anger and there's nothing left of them.
The mighty lion, king of the beasts, roars mightily,
   but when he's toothless he's useless—
No teeth, no prey—and the cubs
   wander off to fend for themselves.

"A word came to me in secret—
   a mere whisper of a word, but I heard it clearly.
It came in a scary dream one night,
   after I had fallen into a deep, deep sleep.
Dread stared me in the face, and Terror.
   I was scared to death—I shook from head to foot.
A spirit glided right in front of me—
   the hair on my head stood on end.

19

I couldn't tell what it was that appeared there—
    a blur . . . and then I heard a muffled voice:

"'How can mere mortals be more righteous than God?
    How can humans be purer than their Creator?
Why, God doesn't even trust his own servants,
    doesn't even cheer his angels,
So how much less these bodies composed of mud,
    fragile as moths?
These bodies of ours are here today and gone tomorrow,
    and no one even notices—gone without a trace.
When the tent stakes are ripped up, the tent collapses—
    we die and are never the wiser for having lived.'

5

DON'T BLAME FATE WHEN THINGS GO WRONG

"Call for help, Job, if you think anyone will answer!
    To which of the holy angels will you turn?
The hot temper of a fool eventually kills him,
    the jealous anger of a simpleton does her in.
I've seen it myself—seen fools putting down roots,
    and then, suddenly, their houses are cursed.
Their children out in the cold, abused and exploited,
    with no one to stick up for them.
Hungry people off the street plunder their harvests,
    cleaning them out completely, taking thorns and all,
    insatiable for everything they have.
Don't blame fate when things go wrong—

trouble doesn't come from nowhere.
It's human! Mortals are born and bred for trouble,
　　as certainly as sparks fly upward.

What a Blessing When God Corrects You!

"If I were in your shoes, I'd go straight to God,
　　I'd throw myself on the mercy of God.
After all, he's famous for great and unexpected acts;
　　there's no end to his surprises.
He gives rain, for instance, across the wide earth,
　　sends water to irrigate the fields.
He raises up the down-and-out,
　　gives firm footing to those sinking in grief.
He aborts the schemes of conniving crooks,
　　so that none of their plots come to term.
He catches the know-it-alls in their conspiracies—
　　all that intricate intrigue swept out with the trash!
Suddenly they're disoriented, plunged into darkness;
　　they can't see to put one foot in front of the other.
But the downtrodden are saved by God,
　　saved from the murderous plots, saved from the iron fist.
And so the poor continue to hope,
　　while injustice is bound and gagged.

"So, what a blessing when God steps in and corrects you!
　　Mind you, don't despise the discipline of Almighty God!
True, he wounds, but he also dresses the wound;
　　the same hand that hurts you, heals you.
From one disaster after another he delivers you;
　　no matter what the calamity, the evil can't touch you—

21

"In famine, he'll keep you from starving,
    in war, from being gutted by the sword.
You'll be protected from vicious gossip
    and live fearless through any catastrophe.
You'll shrug off disaster and famine,
    and stroll fearlessly among wild animals.
You'll be on good terms with rocks and mountains;
    wild animals will become your good friends.
You'll know that your place on earth is safe,
    you'll look over your goods and find nothing amiss.
You'll see your children grow up,
    your family lovely and lissome as orchard grass.
You'll arrive at your grave ripe with many good years,
    like sheaves of golden grain at harvest.

"Yes, this is the way things are—my word of honor!
    Take it to heart and you won't go wrong."

6 JOB REPLIES TO ELIPHAZ

GOD HAS DUMPED THE WORKS ON ME

Job answered:

"If my misery could be weighed,
    if you could pile the whole bitter load on the scales,
It would be heavier than all the sand of the sea!
    Is it any wonder that I'm screaming like a caged cat?
The arrows of God Almighty are in me,

poison arrows—and I'm poisoned all through!
God has dumped the whole works on me.
Donkeys bray and cows moo when they run out of pasture—
so don't expect me to keep quiet in this.
Do you see what God has dished out for me?
It's enough to turn anyone's stomach!
Everything in me is repulsed by it—
it makes me sick.

PRESSED PAST THE LIMITS

"All I want is an answer to one prayer,
a last request to be honored:
Let God step on me—squash me like a bug,
and be done with me for good.
I'd at least have the satisfaction
of not having blasphemed the Holy God,
before being pressed past the limits.
Where's the strength to keep my hopes up?
What future do I have to keep me going?
Do you think I have nerves of steel?
Do you think I'm made of iron?
Do you think I can pull myself up by my bootstraps?
Why, I don't even have any boots!

MY SO-CALLED FRIENDS

"When desperate people give up on God Almighty,
their friends, at least, should stick with them.
But my brothers are fickle as a gulch in the desert—
one day they're gushing with water

23

From melting ice and snow
    cascading out of the mountains,
But by midsummer they're dry,
    gullies baked dry in the sun.
Travelers who spot them and go out of their way for a drink,
    end up in a waterless gulch and die of thirst.
Merchant caravans from Tema see them and expect water,
    tourists from Sheba hope for a cool drink.
They arrive so confident—but what a disappointment!
    They get there, and their faces fall!
And you, my so-called friends, are no better—
        there's nothing to you!
    One look at a hard scene and you shrink in fear.
It's not as though I asked you for anything—
    I didn't ask you for one red cent—
Nor did I beg you to go out on a limb for me.
    So why all this dodging and shuffling?

"Confront me with the truth and I'll shut up,
    show me where I've gone off the track.
Honest words never hurt anyone,
    but what's the point of all this pious bluster?
You pretend to tell me what's wrong with my life,
    but treat my words of anguish as so much hot air.
Are people mere things to you?
    Are friends just items of profit and loss?

"Look me in the eyes!
    Do you think I'd lie to your face?
Think it over—no double-talk!

Think carefully—my integrity is on the line!
Can you detect anything false in what I say?
　　Don't you trust me to discern good from evil?

7

THERE'S NOTHING TO MY LIFE

"Human life is a struggle, isn't it?
　　It's a life sentence to hard labor.
Like field hands longing for quitting time
　　and working stiffs with nothing to hope for but payday,
I'm given a life that meanders and goes nowhere—
　　months of aimlessness, nights of misery!
I go to bed and think, 'How long till I can get up?'
　　I toss and turn as the night drags on—and I'm fed up!
I'm covered with maggots and scabs.
　　My skin gets scaly and hard, then oozes with pus.
My days come and go swifter than the click of knitting
　　　　needles,
　　and then the yarn runs out—an unfinished life!

"God, don't forget that I'm only a puff of air!
　　These eyes have had their last look at goodness.
And your eyes have seen the last of me;
　　even while you're looking, there'll be nothing left to
　　　　look at.
When a cloud evaporates, it's gone for good;
　　those who go to the grave never come back.
They don't return to visit their families;
　　never again will friends drop in for coffee.

25

"And so I'm not keeping one bit of this quiet,
    I'm laying it all out on the table;
      my complaining to high heaven is bitter, but honest.
Are you going to put a muzzle on me,
    the way you quiet the sea and still the storm?
If I say, 'I'm going to bed, then I'll feel better.
    A little nap will lift my spirits,'
You come and so scare me with nightmares
    and frighten me with ghosts
That I'd rather strangle in the bedclothes
    than face this kind of life any longer.
I hate this life! Who needs any more of this?
    Let me alone! There's nothing to my life—it's nothing
      but smoke.

"What are mortals anyway, that you bother with them,
    that you even give them the time of day?
That you check up on them every morning,
    looking in on them to see how they're doing?
Let up on me, will you?
    Can't you even let me spit in peace?
Even suppose I'd sinned—how would that hurt you?
    You're responsible for every human being.
Don't you have better things to do than pick on me?
    Why make a federal case out of me?
Why don't you just forgive my sins
    and start me off with a clean slate?
The way things are going, I'll soon be dead.
    You'll look high and low, but I won't be around."

8 BILDAD'S RESPONSE

Does God Mess Up?

Bildad from Shuah was next to speak:

"How can you keep on talking like this?
    You're talking nonsense, and noisy nonsense at that.
Does God mess up?
    Does God Almighty ever get things backwards?
It's plain that your children sinned against him—
    otherwise, why would God have punished them?
Here's what you must do—and don't put it off any longer:
    Get down on your knees before God Almighty.
If you're as innocent and upright as you say,
    it's not too late—he'll come running;
    he'll set everything right again, reestablish your fortunes.
Even though you're not much right now,
    you'll end up better than ever.

To Hang Your Life From One Thin Thread

"Put the question to our ancestors,
    study what they learned from their ancestors.
For we're newcomers at this, with a lot to learn,
    and not too long to learn it.
So why not let the ancients teach you, tell you what's what,
    instruct you in what they knew from experience?
Can mighty pine trees grow tall without soil?
    Can luscious tomatoes flourish without water?

27

Blossoming flowers look great before they're cut or picked,
    but without soil or water they wither more quickly
        than grass.
That's what happens to all who forget God—
    all their hopes come to nothing.
They hang their life from one thin thread,
    they hitch their fate to a spider web.
One jiggle and the thread breaks,
    one jab and the web collapses.
Or they're like weeds springing up in the sunshine,
    invading the garden,
Spreading everywhere, overtaking the flowers,
    getting a foothold even in the rocks.
But when the gardener rips them out by the roots,
    the garden doesn't miss them one bit.
The sooner the godless are gone, the better;
    then good plants can grow in their place.

"There's no way that God will reject a good person,
    and there is no way he'll help a bad one.
God will let you laugh again;
    you'll raise the roof with shouts of joy,
With your enemies thoroughly discredited,
    their house of cards collapsed."

9   JOB CONTINUES

How Can Mere Mortals Get Right With God?

Job continued by saying:

"So what's new? I know all this.
> The question is, 'How can mere mortals get right
> > with God?'
If we wanted to bring our case before him,
> what chance would we have? Not one in a thousand!
God's wisdom is so deep, God's power so immense,
> who could take him on and come out in one piece?
He moves mountains before they know what's happened,
> flips them on their heads on a whim.
He gives the earth a good shaking up,
> rocks it down to its very foundations.
He tells the sun, 'Don't shine,' and it doesn't;
> he pulls the blinds on the stars.
All by himself he stretches out the heavens
> and strides on the waves of the sea.
He designed the Big Dipper and Orion,
> the Pleiades and Alpha Centauri.
We'll never comprehend all the great things he does;
> his miracle-surprises can't be counted.
Somehow, though he moves right in front of me, I don't
> > see him;
> quietly but surely he's active, and I miss it.
If he steals you blind, who can stop him?
> Who's going to say, 'Hey, what are you doing?'

God doesn't hold back on his anger;
    even dragon-bred monsters cringe before him.

"So how could I ever argue with him,
    construct a defense that would influence God?
Even though I'm innocent I could never prove it;
    I can only throw myself on the Judge's mercy.
If I called on God and he himself answered me,
    then, and only then, would I believe that he'd heard me.
As it is, he knocks me about from pillar to post,
    beating me up, black and blue, for no good reason.
He won't even let me catch my breath,
    piles bitterness upon bitterness.
If it's a question of who's stronger, he wins, hands down!
    If it's a question of justice, who'll serve him the subpoena?
Even though innocent, anything I say incriminates me;
    blameless as I am, my defense just makes me sound worse.

IF GOD'S NOT RESPONSIBLE, WHO IS?

"Believe me, I'm blameless.
    I don't understand what's going on.
    I hate my life!
Since either way it ends up the same, I can only conclude
    that God destroys the good right along with the bad.
When calamity hits and brings sudden death,
    he folds his arms, aloof from the despair of the innocent.
He lets the wicked take over running the world,
    he installs judges who can't tell right from wrong.
    If he's not responsible, who is?

30

"My time is short—what's left of my life races off
    too fast for me to even glimpse the good.
My life is going fast, like a ship under full sail,
    like an eagle plummeting to its prey.
Even if I say, 'I'll put all this behind me,
    I'll look on the bright side and force a smile,'
All these troubles would still be like grit in my gut
    since it's clear you're not going to let up.
The verdict has already been handed down—'Guilty!'—
    so what's the use of protests or appeals?
Even if I scrub myself all over
    and wash myself with the strongest soap I can find,
It wouldn't last—you'd push me into a pigpen, or worse,
    so nobody could stand me for the stink.

"God and I are not equals; I can't bring a case against him.
    We'll never enter a courtroom as peers.
How I wish we had an arbitrator
    to step in and let me get on with life—
To break God's death grip on me,
    to free me from this terror so I could breathe again.
Then I'd speak up and state my case boldly.
    As things stand, there is no way I can do it.

10

To Find Some Skeleton in My Closet

"I can't stand my life—I hate it!
    I'm putting it all out on the table,

31

all the bitterness of my life—I'm holding back
    nothing."

Job prayed:

"Here's what I want to say:
Don't, God, bring in a verdict of guilty
    without letting me know the charges you're bringing.
How does this fit into what you once called 'good'—
    giving me a hard time, spurning me,
    a life you shaped by your very own hands,
    and then blessing the plots of the wicked?
You don't look at things the way we mortals do.
    You're not taken in by appearances, are you?
Unlike us, you're not working against a deadline.
    You have all eternity to work things out.
So what's this all about, anyway—this compulsion
    to dig up some dirt, to find some skeleton in my closet?
You know good and well I'm not guilty.
    You also know no one can help me.

"You made me like a handcrafted piece of pottery—
    and now are you going to smash me to pieces?
Don't you remember how beautifully you worked my clay?
    Will you reduce me now to a mud pie?
Oh, that marvel of conception as you stirred together
    semen and ovum—
What a miracle of skin and bone,
    muscle and brain!
You gave me life itself, and incredible love.
    You watched and guarded every breath I took.

32

"But you never told me about this part.
    I should have known that there was more to it—
That if I so much as missed a step, you'd notice and pounce,
    wouldn't let me get by with a thing.
If I'm truly guilty, I'm doomed.
    But if I'm innocent, it's no better—I'm still doomed.
My belly is full of bitterness.
    I'm up to my ears in a swamp of affliction.
I try to make the best of it, try to brave it out,
    but you're too much for me,
    relentless, like a lion on the prowl.
You line up fresh witnesses against me.
    You compound your anger
    and pile on the grief and pain!

"So why did you have me born?
    I wish no one had ever laid eyes on me!
I wish I'd never lived—a stillborn,
    buried without ever having breathed.
Isn't it time to call it quits on my life?
    Can't you let up, and let me smile just once
Before I die and am buried,
    before I'm nailed into my coffin, sealed in the ground,
And banished for good to the land of the dead,
    blind in the final dark?"

11   ZOPHAR'S COUNSEL

HOW WISDOM LOOKS FROM THE INSIDE

Now it was the turn of Zophar from Naamath:

"What a flood of words! Shouldn't we put a stop to it?
  Should this kind of loose talk be permitted?
Job, do you think you can carry on like this and we'll say
      nothing?
  That we'll let you rail and mock and not step in?
You claim, 'My doctrine is sound
  and my conduct impeccable.'
How I wish God would give you a piece of his mind,
  tell you what's what!
I wish he'd show you how wisdom looks from the inside,
  for true wisdom is mostly 'inside.'
But you can be sure of this,
  you haven't gotten half of what you deserve.

"Do you think you can explain the mystery of God?
  Do you think you can diagram God Almighty?
God is far higher than you can imagine,
  far deeper than you can comprehend,
Stretching farther than earth's horizons,
  far wider than the endless ocean.
If he happens along, throws you in jail
  then hauls you into court, can you do anything about it?
He sees through vain pretensions,
    spots evil a long way off—
    no one pulls the wool over *his* eyes!

Hollow men, hollow women, will wise up
    about the same time mules learn to talk.

REACH OUT TO GOD

"Still, if you set your heart on God
    and reach out to him,
If you scrub your hands of sin
    and refuse to entertain evil in your home,
You'll be able to face the world unashamed
    and keep a firm grip on life, guiltless and fearless.
You'll forget your troubles;
    they'll be like old, faded photographs.
Your world will be washed in sunshine,
    every shadow dispersed by dayspring.
Full of hope, you'll relax, confident again;
    you'll look around, sit back, and take it easy.
Expansive, without a care in the world,
    you'll be hunted out by many for your blessing.
But the wicked will see none of this.
    They're headed down a dead-end road
    with nothing to look forward to—nothing."

12   JOB ANSWERS ZOPHAR

PUT YOUR EAR TO THE EARTH

Job answered:

"I'm sure you speak for all the experts,
    and when you die there'll be no one left to tell us how to live.

35

But don't forget that I also have a brain—
    I don't intend to play second fiddle to you.
    It doesn't take an expert to know these things.

"I'm ridiculed by my friends:
    'So that's the man who had conversations with God!'
Ridiculed without mercy:
    'Look at the man who never did wrong!'
It's easy for the well-to-do to point their fingers in blame,
    for the well-fixed to pour scorn on the strugglers.
Crooks reside safely in high-security houses,
    insolent blasphemers live in luxury;
        they've bought and paid for a god who'll protect them.

"But ask the animals what they think—let them teach you;
    let the birds tell you what's going on.
Put your ear to the earth—learn the basics.
    Listen—the fish in the ocean will tell you their stories.
Isn't it clear that they all know and agree
    that GOD is sovereign, that he holds all things in his hand—
Every living soul, yes,
    every breathing creature?
Isn't this all just common sense,
    as common as the sense of taste?
Do you think the elderly have a corner on wisdom,
    that you have to grow old before you understand life?

FROM GOD WE LEARN HOW TO LIVE
"True wisdom and real power belong to God;
    from him we learn how to live,
    and also what to live for.

If he tears something down, it's down for good;
    if he locks people up, they're locked up for good.
If he holds back the rain, there's a drought;
    if he lets it loose, there's a flood.
Strength and success belong to God;
    both deceived and deceiver must answer to him.
He strips experts of their vaunted credentials,
    exposes judges as witless fools.
He divests kings of their royal garments,
    then ties a rag around their waists.
He strips priests of their robes,
    and fires high officials from their jobs.
He forces trusted sages to keep silence,
    deprives elders of their good sense and wisdom.
He dumps contempt on famous people,
    disarms the strong and mighty.
He shines a spotlight into caves of darkness,
    hauls deepest darkness into the noonday sun.
He makes nations rise and then fall,
    builds up some and abandons others.
He robs world leaders of their reason,
    and sends them off into no man's land.
They grope in the dark without a clue,
    lurching and staggering like drunks.

13

I'M TAKING MY CASE TO GOD

"Yes, I've seen all this with my own eyes,
    heard and understood it with my very own ears.

Everything you know, I know,
    so I'm not taking a back seat to any of you.
I'm taking my case straight to God Almighty;
    I've had it with you—I'm going directly to God.
You graffiti my life with lies.
    You're a bunch of pompous quacks!
I wish you'd shut your mouths—
    silence is your only claim to wisdom.

"Listen now while I make my case,
    consider my side of things for a change.
Or are you going to keep on lying 'to do God a service'?
    to make up stories 'to get him off the hook'?
Why do you always take his side?
    Do you think he needs a lawyer to defend himself?
How would you fare if you were in the dock?
    Your lies might convince a jury—but would they convince
        God?
He'd reprimand you on the spot
    if he detected a bias in your witness.
Doesn't his splendor put you in awe?
    Aren't you afraid to speak cheap lies before him?
Your wise sayings are knickknack wisdom,
    good for nothing but gathering dust.

"So hold your tongue while I have my say,
    then I'll take whatever I have coming to me.
Why do I go out on a limb like this
    and take my life in my hands?
Because even if he killed me, I'd keep on hoping.

I'd defend my innocence to the very end.
Just wait, this is going to work out for the best—my salvation!
    If I were guilt-stricken do you think I'd be doing this—
    laying myself on the line before God?
You'd better pay attention to what I'm telling you,
    listen carefully with both ears.
Now that I've laid out my defense,
    I'm sure that I'll be acquitted.
Can anyone prove charges against me?
    I've said my piece. I rest my case.

WHY DOES GOD STAY HIDDEN AND SILENT?

"Please, God, I have two requests;
    grant them so I'll know I count with you:
First, lay off the afflictions;
    the terror is too much for me.
Second, address me directly so I can answer you,
    or let me speak and then you answer me.
How many sins have been charged against me?
    Show me the list—how bad is it?
Why do you stay hidden and silent?
    Why treat me like I'm your enemy?
Why kick me around like an old tin can?
    Why beat a dead horse?
You compile a long list of mean things about me,
    even hold me accountable for the sins of my youth.
You hobble me so I can't move about.
    You watch every move I make,
    and brand me as a dangerous character.

39

"Like something rotten, human life fast decomposes,
   like a moth-eaten shirt or a mildewed blouse.

14

IF WE DIE, WILL WE LIVE AGAIN?

"We're all adrift in the same boat:
   too few days, too many troubles.
We spring up like wildflowers in the desert and then wilt,
   transient as the shadow of a cloud.
Do you occupy your time with such fragile wisps?
   Why even bother hauling me into court?
There's nothing much to us to start with;
   how do you expect us to amount to anything?
Mortals have a limited life span.
   You've already decided how long we'll live—
   you set the boundary and no one can cross it.
So why not give us a break? Ease up!
   Even ditchdiggers get occasional days off.
For a tree there is always hope.
   Chop it down and it still has a chance—
   its roots can put out fresh sprouts.
Even if its roots are old and gnarled,
   its stump long dormant,
At the first whiff of water it comes to life,
   buds and grows like a sapling.
But men and women? They die and stay dead.
   They breathe their last, and that's it.
Like lakes and rivers that have dried up,

parched reminders of what once was,
So mortals lie down and never get up,
    never wake up again—never.
Why don't you just bury me alive,
    get me out of the way until your anger cools?
But don't leave me there!
    Set a date when you'll see me again.
If we humans die, will we live again? That's my question.
    All through these difficult days I keep hoping,
        waiting for the final change—for resurrection!
Homesick with longing for the creature you made,
    you'll call—and I'll answer!
You'll watch over every step I take,
    but you won't keep track of my missteps.
My sins will be stuffed in a sack
    and thrown into the sea—sunk in deep ocean.

"Meanwhile, mountains wear down
    and boulders break up,
Stones wear smooth
    and soil erodes,
        as you relentlessly grind down our hope.
You're too much for us.
    As always, you get the last word.
We don't like it and our faces show it,
    but you send us off anyway.
If our children do well for themselves, we never know it;
    if they do badly, we're spared the hurt.
Body and soul, that's it for us—
    a lifetime of pain, a lifetime of sorrow."

41

15 ELIPHAZ ATTACKS AGAIN

YOU TRIVIALIZE RELIGION

Eliphaz of Teman spoke a second time:

"If you were truly wise, would you sound so much like
      a windbag,
    belching hot air?
Would you talk nonsense in the middle of a serious argument,
    babbling baloney?
Look at you! You trivialize religion,
    turn spiritual conversation into empty gossip.
It's your sin that taught you to talk this way.
    You chose an education in fraud.
Your own words have exposed your guilt.
    It's nothing I've said—you've incriminated yourself!
Do you think you're the first person to have to deal with these
      things?
    Have you been around as long as the hills?
Were you listening in when God planned all this?
    Do you think you're the only one who knows anything?
What do you know that we don't know?
    What insights do you have that we've missed?
Gray beards and white hair back us up—
    old folks who've been around a lot longer than you.
Are God's promises not enough for you,
    spoken so gently and tenderly?
Why do you let your emotions take over,
    lashing out and spitting fire,

Pitting your whole being against God
    by letting words like this come out of your mouth?
Do you think it's possible for any mere mortal to be sinless in
        God's sight,
    for anyone born of a human mother to get it all together?
Why, God can't even trust his holy angels.
    He sees the flaws in the very heavens themselves,
So how much less we humans, smelly and foul,
    who lap up evil like water?

ALWAYS AT ODDS WITH GOD
"I've a thing or two to tell you, so listen up!
    I'm letting you in on my views;
It's what wise men and women have always taught,
    holding nothing back from what *they* were taught
By their parents, back in the days
    when they had this land all to themselves:
Those who live by their own rules, not God's, can expect
        nothing but trouble,
    and the longer they live, the worse it gets.
Every little sound terrifies them.
    Just when they think they have it made, disaster strikes.
They despair of things ever getting better—
    they're on the list of people for whom things always turn
        out for the worst.
They wander here and there,
    never knowing where the next meal is coming from—
    every day is doomsday!
They live in constant terror,
    always with their backs up against the wall

Because they insist on shaking their fists at God,
    defying God Almighty to his face,
Always and ever at odds with God,
    always on the defensive.

"Even if they're the picture of health,
    trim and fit and youthful,
They'll end up living in a ghost town
    sleeping in a hovel not fit for a dog,
    a ramshackle shack.
They'll never get ahead,
    never amount to a hill of beans.
And then death—don't think they'll escape that!
    They'll end up shriveled weeds,
    brought down by a puff of God's breath.
There's a lesson here: Whoever invests in lies,
    gets lies for interest,
Paid in full before the due date.
    Some investment!
They'll be like fruit frost-killed before it ripens,
    like buds sheared off before they bloom.
The godless are fruitless—a barren crew;
    a life built on bribes goes up in smoke.
They have sex with sin and give birth to evil.
    Their lives are wombs for breeding deceit."

16 JOB DEFENDS HIMSELF

IF YOU WERE IN MY SHOES

Then Job defended himself:

"I've had all I can take of your talk.
  What a bunch of miserable comforters!
Is there no end to your windbag speeches?
  What's your problem that you go on and on like this?
If you were in my shoes,
  I could talk just like you.
I could put together a terrific harangue
  and really let you have it.
But I'd never do that. I'd console and comfort,
  make things better, not worse!

"When I speak up, I feel no better;
  if I say nothing, that doesn't help either.
I feel worn down.
  God, you have wasted me totally—me and my family!
You've shriveled me like a dried prune,
  showing the world that you're against me.
My gaunt face stares back at me from the mirror,
  a mute witness to your treatment of me.
Your anger tears at me,
  your teeth rip me to shreds,
    your eyes burn holes in me—God, my enemy!
People take one look at me and gasp.
  Contemptuous, they slap me around
    and gang up against me.

And God just stands there and lets them do it,
    lets wicked people do what they want with me.
I was contentedly minding my business when God beat me up.
    He grabbed me by the neck and threw me around.
He set me up as his target,
    then rounded up archers to shoot at me.
Merciless, they shot me full of arrows;
    bitter bile poured from my gut to the ground.
He burst in on me, onslaught after onslaught,
    charging me like a mad bull.

"I sewed myself a shroud and wore it like a shirt;
    I lay face down in the dirt.
Now my face is blotched red from weeping;
    look at the dark shadows under my eyes,
Even though I've never hurt a soul
    and my prayers are sincere!

THE ONE WHO REPRESENTS MORTALS BEFORE GOD

"Oh Earth, don't cover up the wrong done to me!
    Don't muffle my cry!
There must be Someone in heaven who knows the truth
       about me,
    in highest heaven, some Attorney who can clear my
       name—
My Champion, my Friend,
    while I'm weeping my eyes out before God.
I appeal to the One who represents mortals before God
    as a neighbor stands up for a neighbor.

"Only a few years are left
    before I set out on the road of no return.

17

"My spirit is broken,
    my days used up,
    my grave dug and waiting.
See how these mockers close in on me?
    How long do I have to put up with their insolence?

"O God, pledge your support for me.
    Give it to me in writing, with your signature.
    You're the only one who can do it!
These people are so useless!
    You know firsthand how stupid they can be.
    You wouldn't let them have the last word, would you?
Those who betray their own friends
    leave a legacy of abuse to their children.

"God, you've made me the talk of the town—
    people spit in my face;
I can hardly see from crying so much;
    I'm nothing but skin and bones.
Decent people can't believe what they're seeing;
    the good-hearted wake up and insist I've given up on God.

"But principled people hold tight, keep a firm grip on life,
    sure that their clean, pure hands will get stronger and
        stronger!

"Maybe you'd all like to start over,
    to try it again, the bunch of you.
So far I haven't come across one scrap
    of wisdom in anything you've said.
My life's about over. All my plans are smashed,
    all my hopes are snuffed out—
My hope that night would turn into day,
    my hope that dawn was about to break.
If all I have to look forward to is a home in the graveyard,
    if my only hope for comfort is a well-built coffin,
If a family reunion means going six feet under,
    and the only family that shows up is worms,
Do you call that hope?
    Who on earth could find any hope in that?
No. If hope and I are to be buried together,
    I suppose you'll all come to the double funeral!"

18   BILDAD'S SECOND ATTACK

PLUNGED FROM LIGHT INTO DARKNESS

Bildad from Shuhah chimed in:

"How monotonous these word games are getting!
    Get serious! We need to get down to business.
Why do you treat your friends like slow-witted animals?
    You look down on us as if we don't know anything.
Why are you working yourself up like this?
    Do you want the world redesigned to suit you?
    Should reality be suspended to accommodate you?

"Here's the rule: The light of the wicked is put out.
    Their flame dies down and is extinguished.
Their house goes dark—
    every lamp in the place goes out.
Their strong strides weaken, falter;
    they stumble into their own traps.
They get all tangled up
    in their own red tape,
Their feet are grabbed and caught,
    their necks in a noose.
They trip on ropes they've hidden,
    and fall into pits they've dug themselves.
Terrors come at them from all sides.
    They run helter-skelter.
The hungry grave is ready
    to gobble them up for supper,
To lay them out for a gourmet meal,
    a treat for ravenous Death.
They are snatched from their home sweet home
    and marched straight to the death house.
Their lives go up in smoke;
    acid rain soaks their ruins.
Their roots rot
    and their branches wither.
They'll never again be remembered—
    nameless in unmarked graves.
They are plunged from light into darkness,
    banished from the world.
And they leave empty-handed—not one single child—
    nothing to show for their life on this earth.

Westerners are aghast at their fate,
    easterners are horrified:
'Oh no! So this is what happens to perverse people.
    This is how the God-ignorant end up!'"

19   JOB ANSWERS BILDAD

I Call for Help and No One Bothers

Job answered:

"How long are you going to keep battering away at me,
    pounding me with these harangues?
Time after time after time you jump all over me.
    Do you have no conscience, abusing me like this?
Even if I have, somehow or other, gotten off the track,
    what business is that of yours?
Why do you insist on putting me down,
    using my troubles as a stick to beat me?
Tell it to God—he's the one behind all this,
    he's the one who dragged me into this mess.

"Look at me—I shout 'Murder!' and I'm ignored;
    I call for help and no one bothers to stop.
God threw a barricade across my path—I'm stymied;
    he turned out all the lights—I'm stuck in the dark.
He destroyed my reputation,
    robbed me of all self-respect.
He tore me apart piece by piece—I'm ruined!
    Then he yanked out hope by the roots.

He's angry with me—oh, how he's angry!
    He treats me like his worst enemy.
He has launched a major campaign against me,
    using every weapon he can think of,
    coming at me from all sides at once.

I Know That God Lives

"God alienated my family from me;
    everyone who knows me avoids me.
My relatives and friends have all left;
    houseguests forget I ever existed.
The servant girls treat me like a bum off the street,
    look at me like they've never seen me before.
I call my attendant and he ignores me,
    ignores me even though I plead with him.
My wife can't stand to be around me anymore.
    I'm repulsive to my family.
Even street urchins despise me;
    when I come out, they taunt and jeer.
Everyone I've ever been close to abhors me;
    my dearest loved ones reject me.
I'm nothing but a bag of bones;
    my life hangs by a thread.

"Oh, friends, dear friends, take pity on me.
    God has come down hard on me!
Do you have to be hard on me too?
    Don't you ever tire of abusing me?

51

"If only my words were written in a book—
  better yet, chiseled in stone!
Still, I know that God lives—the One who gives me back my
      life—
  and eventually he'll take his stand on earth.
And I'll see him—even though I get skinned alive!—
  see God myself, with my very own eyes.
  Oh, how I long for that day!

"If you're thinking, 'How can we get through to him,
  get him to see that his trouble is all his own fault?'
Forget it. Start worrying about *yourselves*.
  Worry about your own sins and God's coming judgment,
  for judgment is most certainly on the way."

ZOPHAR ATTACKS JOB—
20 THE SECOND ROUND

SAVORING EVIL AS A DELICACY

Zophar from Naamath again took his turn:

"I can't believe what I'm hearing!
  You've put my teeth on edge, my stomach in a knot.
How dare you insult my intelligence like this!
  Well, here's a piece of my mind!

"Don't you even know the basics,
  how things have been since the earliest days,
  when Adam and Eve were first placed on earth?

The good times of the wicked are short-lived;
    godless joy is only momentary.
The evil might become world famous,
    strutting at the head of the celebrity parade,
But still end up in a pile of dung.
        Acquaintances look at them with disgust and say,
            'What's that?'
They fly off like a dream that can't be remembered,
    like a shadowy illusion that vanishes in the light.
Though once notorious public figures, now they're nobodies,
    unnoticed, whether they come or go.
Their children will go begging on skid row,
    and they'll have to give back their ill-gotten gain.
Right in the prime of life,
    and youthful and vigorous, they'll die.

"They savor evil as a delicacy,
    roll it around on their tongues,
Prolong the flavor, a dalliance in decadence—
    real gourmets of evil!
But then they get stomach cramps,
    a bad case of food poisoning.
They gag on all that rich food;
    God makes them vomit it up.
They gorge on evil, make a diet of that poison—
    a deadly diet—and it kills them.
No quiet picnics for them beside gentle streams
    with fresh-baked bread and cheese, and tall, cool drinks.
They spit out their food half-chewed,
    unable to relax and enjoy anything they've worked for.

53

And why? Because they exploited the poor,
    took what never belonged to them.

"Such God-denying people are never content with what they
      have or who they are;
    their greed drives them relentlessly.
They plunder everything
    but they can't hold on to any of it.
Just when they think they have it all, disaster strikes;
    they're served up a plate full of misery.
When they've filled their bellies with that,
    God gives them a taste of his anger,
    and they get to chew on that for a while.
As they run for their lives from one disaster,
    they run smack into another.
They're knocked around from pillar to post,
    beaten to within an inch of their lives.
They're trapped in a house of horrors,
    and see their loot disappear down a black hole.
Their lives are a total loss—
    not a penny to their name, not so much as a bean.
God will strip them of their sin-soaked clothes
    and hang their dirty laundry out for all to see.
Life is a complete wipe-out for them,
    nothing surviving God's wrath.
There! That's God's blueprint for the wicked—
    what they have to look forward to."

21 JOB'S RESPONSE

WHY DO THE WICKED HAVE IT SO GOOD?

Job replied:

"Now listen to me carefully, please listen,
      at least do me the favor of listening.
Put up with me while I have my say—
      then you can mock me later to your heart's content.

"It's not *you* I'm complaining to—it's *God*.
      Is it any wonder I'm getting fed up with his silence?
Take a good look at me. Aren't you appalled by what's
            happened?
      No! Don't say anything. I can do without your comments.
When I look back, I go into shock,
      my body is racked with spasms.
Why do the wicked have it so good,
      live to a ripe old age and get rich?
They get to see their children succeed,
      get to watch and enjoy their grandchildren.
Their homes are peaceful and free from fear;
      they never experience God's disciplining rod.
Their bulls breed with great vigor
      and their cows calve without fail.
They send their children out to play
      and watch them frolic like spring lambs.
They make music with fiddles and flutes,
      have good times singing and dancing.
They have a long life on easy street,
      and die painlessly in their sleep.

They say to God, 'Get lost!
  We've no interest in you or your ways.
Why should we have dealings with God Almighty?
  What's there in it for us?'
But they're wrong, dead wrong—they're not gods.
  It's beyond me how they can carry on like this!

"Still, how often does it happen that the wicked fail,
  or disaster strikes,
  or they get their just deserts?
How often are they blown away by bad luck?
  Not very often.
You might say, 'God is saving up the punishment for their
    children.'
  I say, 'Give it to them right now so they'll know what
    they've done!'
They deserve to experience the effects of their evil,
  feel the full force of God's wrath firsthand.
What do they care what happens to their families
  after they're safely tucked away in the grave?

FANCY FUNERALS WITH ALL THE TRIMMINGS

"But who are we to tell God how to run his affairs?
  He's dealing with matters that are way over our heads.
Some people die in the prime of life,
  with everything going for them—
  fat and sassy.
Others die bitter and bereft,
  never getting a taste of happiness.

They're laid out side by side in the cemetery,
    where the worms can't tell one from the other.

"I'm not deceived. I know what you're up to,
    the plans you're cooking up to bring me down.
Naively you claim that the castles of tyrants fall to pieces,
    that the achievements of the wicked collapse.
Have you ever asked world travelers how they see it?
    Have you not listened to their stories
Of evil men and women who got off scot-free,
    who never had to pay for their wickedness?
Did anyone ever confront them with their crimes?
    Did they ever have to face the music?
Not likely—they're given fancy funerals
    with all the trimmings,
Gently lowered into expensive graves,
    with everyone telling lies about how wonderful they were.

"So how do you expect me to get any comfort from your
        nonsense?
    Your so-called comfort is a tissue of lies."

22   ELIPHAZ ATTACKS JOB—
THE THIRD ROUND

COME TO TERMS WITH GOD

Once again Eliphaz the Temanite took up his theme:

"Are any of us strong enough to give God a hand,
    or smart enough to give him advice?

57

So what if you were righteous—would God Almighty even
notice?
Even if you gave a perfect performance, do you think he'd
applaud?
Do you think it's because he cares about your purity
that he's disciplining you, putting you on the spot?
Hardly! It's because you're a first-class moral failure,
because there's no end to your sins.
When people came to you for help,
you took the shirts off their backs, exploited their
helplessness.
You wouldn't so much as give a drink to the thirsty,
or food, not even a scrap, to the hungry.
And there you sat, strong and honored by everyone,
surrounded by immense wealth!
You turned poor widows away from your door;
heartless, you crushed orphans.
Now *you're* the one trapped in terror, paralyzed by fear.
Suddenly the tables have turned!
How do you like living in the dark, sightless,
up to your neck in flood waters?

"You agree, don't you, that God is in charge?
He runs the universe—just look at the stars!
Yet you dare raise questions: 'What does God know?
From that distance and darkness, how can he judge?
He roams the heavens wrapped in clouds,
so how can he see us?'

"Are you going to persist in that tired old line
that wicked men and women have always used?

Where did it get them? They died young,
    flash floods sweeping them off to their doom.
They told God, 'Get lost!
    What good is God Almighty to us?'
And yet it was God who gave them everything they had.
    It's beyond me how they can carry on like this!

"Good people see bad people crash, and call for a celebration.
    Relieved, they crow,
'At last! Our enemies—wiped out.
    Everything they had and stood for is up in smoke!'

"Give in to God, come to terms with him
    and everything will turn out just fine.
Let him tell you what to do;
    take his words to heart.
Come back to God Almighty
    and he'll rebuild your life.
Clean house of everything evil.
    Relax your grip on your money
    and abandon your gold-plated luxury.
God Almighty will be your treasure,
    more wealth than you can imagine.

"You'll take delight in God, the Mighty One,
    and look to him joyfully, boldly.
You'll pray to him and he'll listen;
    he'll help you do what you've promised.
You'll decide what you want and it will happen;

your life will be bathed in light.
To those who feel low you'll say, 'Chin up! Be brave!'
    and God will save them.
Yes, even the guilty will escape,
    escape through God's grace in your life."

23   JOB'S DEFENSE

I'M COMPLETELY IN THE DARK

Job replied:

"I'm not letting up—I'm standing my ground.
    My complaint is legitimate.
God has no right to treat me like this—
    it isn't fair!
If I knew where on earth to find him,
    I'd go straight to him.
I'd lay my case before him face-to-face,
    give him all my arguments firsthand.
I'd find out exactly what he's thinking,
    discover what's going on in his head.
Do you think he'd dismiss me or bully me?
    No, he'd take me seriously.
He'd see a straight-living man standing before him;
    my Judge would acquit me for good of all charges.

"I travel East looking for him—I find no one;
    then West, but not a trace;

I go North, but he's hidden his tracks;
>then South, but not even a glimpse.

"But he knows where I am and what I've done.
>He can cross-examine me all he wants, and I'll pass the test
>>with honors.
I've followed him closely, my feet in his footprints,
>not once swerving from his way.
I've obeyed every word he's spoken,
>and not just obeyed his advice—I've *treasured* it.

"But he is singular and sovereign. Who can argue with him?
>He does what he wants, when he wants to.
He'll complete in detail what he's decided about me,
>and whatever else he determines to do.
Is it any wonder that I dread meeting him?
>Whenever I think about it, I get scared all over again.
God makes my heart sink!
>God Almighty gives me the shudders!
I'm completely in the dark,
>I can't see my hand in front of my face.

24

An Illusion of Security

"But if Judgment Day isn't hidden from the Almighty,
>why are we kept in the dark?
There are people out there getting by with murder—
>stealing and lying and cheating.

They rip off the poor
    and exploit the unfortunate,
Push the helpless into the ditch,
    bully the weak so that they fear for their lives.
The poor, like stray dogs and cats,
    scavenge for food in back alleys.
They sort through the garbage of the rich,
    eke out survival on handouts.
Homeless, they shiver through cold nights on the street;
    they've no place to lay their heads.
Exposed to the weather, wet and frozen,
    they huddle in makeshift shelters.
Nursing mothers have their babies snatched from them;
    the infants of the poor are kidnapped and sold.
They go about patched and threadbare;
    even the hard workers go hungry.
No matter how back-breaking their labor,
    they can never make ends meet.
People are dying right and left, groaning in torment.
    The wretched cry out for help
    and God does nothing, acts like nothing's wrong!

"Then there are those who avoid light at all costs,
    who scorn the light-filled path.
When the sun goes down, the murderer gets up—
    kills the poor and robs the defenseless.
Sexual predators can't wait for nightfall,
    thinking, 'No one can see us now.'
Burglars do their work at night,
    but keep well out of sight through the day.

They want nothing to do with light.
Deep darkness is morning for that bunch;
>they make the terrors of darkness their companions
>>in crime.

"They are scraps of wood floating on the water—
>useless, cursed junk, good for nothing.
As surely as snow melts under the hot, summer sun,
>sinners disappear in the grave.
The womb has forgotten them, worms have relished them—
>nothing that is evil lasts.
Unscrupulous,
>they prey on those less fortunate.
However much they strut and flex their muscles,
>there's nothing to them. They're hollow.
They may have an illusion of security,
>but God has his eye on them.
They may get their brief successes,
>but then it's over, nothing to show for it.
Like yesterday's newspaper,
>they're used to wrap up the garbage.
You're free to try to prove me a liar,
>but you won't be able to do it."

25 BILDAD'S THIRD ATTACK

EVEN THE STARS AREN'T PERFECT IN GOD'S EYES

Bildad the Shuhite again attacked Job:

"God is sovereign, God is fearsome—
>everything in the cosmos fits and works in his plan.

Can anyone count his angel armies?
> Is there any place where his light doesn't shine?
How can a mere mortal presume to stand up to God?
> How can an ordinary person pretend to be guiltless?
Why, even the moon has its flaws,
> even the stars aren't perfect in God's eyes,
So how much less, plain men and women—
> slugs and maggots by comparison!"

26   JOB'S DEFENSE

GOD SETS A BOUNDARY BETWEEN LIGHT AND DARKNESS

Job answered:

"Well, you've certainly been a great help to a helpless man!
> You came to the rescue just in the nick of time!
What wonderful advice you've given to a mixed-up man!
> What amazing insights you've provided!
Where in the world did you learn all this?
> How did you become so inspired!

"All the buried dead are in torment,
> and all who've been drowned in the deep, deep sea.
Hell is ripped open before God,
> graveyards dug up and exposed.
He spreads the skies over unformed space,
> hangs the earth out in empty space.
He pours water into cumulus cloud-bags
> and the bags don't burst.

He makes the moon wax and wane,
    putting it through its phases.
He draws the horizon out over the ocean,
    sets a boundary between light and darkness.
Thunder crashes and rumbles in the skies.
    Listen! It's God raising his voice!
By his power he stills sea storms,
    by his wisdom he tames sea monsters.
With one breath he clears the sky,
    with one finger he crushes the sea serpent.
And this is only the beginning,
    a mere whisper of his rule.
    Whatever would we do if he *really* raised his voice!"

27

No Place to Hide

Having waited for Zophar, Job now resumed his defense:

"God-Alive! He's denied me justice!
    God Almighty! He's ruined my life!
But for as long as I draw breath,
    and for as long as God breathes life into me,
I refuse to say one word that isn't true.
    I refuse to confess to any charge that's false.
There is no way I'll ever agree to your accusations.
    I'll not deny my integrity even if it costs me my life.
I'm holding fast to my integrity and not loosening my grip—
    and, believe me, I'll never regret it.

"Let my enemy be exposed as wicked!
    Let my adversary be proven guilty!
What hope do people without God have when life is cut short?
    when God puts an end to life?
Do you think God will listen to their cry for help
    when disaster hits?
What interest have they ever shown in the Almighty?
    Have they ever been known to pray before?

"I've given you a clear account of God in action,
    suppressed nothing regarding God Almighty.
The evidence is right before you. You can all see it for
        yourselves,
    so why do you keep talking nonsense?

"I'll quote your own words back to you:

"'This is how God treats the wicked,
    this is what evil people can expect from God Almighty:
Their children—all of them—will die violent deaths;
    they'll never have enough bread to put on the table.
They'll be wiped out by the plague,
    and none of the widows will shed a tear when they're gone.
Even if they make a lot of money
    and are resplendent in the latest fashions,
It's the good who will end up wearing the clothes
    and the decent who will divide up the money.
They build elaborate houses
    that won't survive a single winter.
They go to bed wealthy
    and wake up poor.

Terrors pour in on them like flash floods—
    a tornado snatches them away in the middle of the night,
A cyclone sweeps them up—gone!
    Not a trace of them left, not even a footprint.
Catastrophes relentlessly pursue them;
    they run this way and that, but there's no place to hide—
Pummeled by the weather,
    blown to kingdom come by the storm.'

28

WHERE DOES WISDOM COME FROM?

"We all know how silver seams the rocks,
    we've seen the stuff from which gold is refined,
We're aware of how iron is dug out of the ground
    and copper is smelted from rock.
Miners penetrate the earth's darkness,
    searching the roots of the mountains for ore,
    digging away in the suffocating darkness.
Far from civilization, far from the traffic,
    they cut a shaft,
    and are lowered into it by ropes.
Earth's surface is a field for grain,
    but its depths are a forge
Firing sapphires from stones
    and chiseling gold from rocks.
Vultures are blind to its riches,
    hawks never lay eyes on it.
Wild animals are oblivious to it,
    lions don't know it's there.

Miners hammer away at the rock,
    they uproot the mountains.
They tunnel through the rock
    and find all kinds of beautiful gems.
They discover the origins of rivers,
    and bring earth's secrets to light.

"But where, oh where, will they find Wisdom?
    Where does Insight hide?
Mortals don't have a clue,
    haven't the slightest idea where to look.
Earth's depths say, 'It's not here';
    ocean deeps echo, 'Never heard of it.'
It can't be bought with the finest gold;
    no amount of silver can get it.
Even famous Ophir gold can't buy it,
    not even diamonds and sapphires.
Neither gold nor emeralds are comparable;
    extravagant jewelry can't touch it.
Pearl necklaces and ruby bracelets—why bother?
    None of this is even a down payment on Wisdom!
Pile gold and African diamonds as high as you will,
    they can't hold a candle to Wisdom.

"So where does Wisdom come from?
    And where does Insight live?
It can't be found by looking, no matter
    how deep you dig, no matter how high you fly.
If you search through the graveyard and question the dead,
    they say, 'We've only heard rumors of it.'

"God alone knows the way to Wisdom,
    he knows the exact place to find it.
He knows where everything is on earth,
    he sees everything under heaven.
After he commanded the winds to blow
    and measured out the waters,
Arranged for the rain
    and set off explosions of thunder and lightning,
He focused on Wisdom,
    made sure it was all set and tested and ready.
Then he addressed the human race: 'Here it is!
    Fear-of-the-Lord—that's Wisdom,
    and Insight means shunning evil.'"

29

WHEN GOD WAS STILL BY MY SIDE

Job now resumed his response:

"Oh, how I long for the good old days,
    when God took such very good care of me.
He always held a lamp before me
    and I walked through the dark by its light.
Oh, how I miss those golden years
    when God's friendship graced my home,
When the Mighty One was still by my side
    and my children were all around me,
When everything was going my way,
    and nothing seemed too difficult.

"When I walked downtown
    and sat with my friends in the public square,
Young and old greeted me with respect;
    I was honored by everyone in town.
When I spoke, everyone listened;
    they hung on my every word.
People who knew me, spoke well of me;
    my reputation went ahead of me.
I was known for helping people in trouble
    and standing up for those who were down on their luck.
The dying blessed me,
    and the bereaved were cheered by my visits.
All my dealings with people were good.
    I was known for being fair to everyone I met.
I was eyes to the blind
    and feet to the lame,
Father to the needy,
    and champion of abused aliens.
I grabbed street thieves by the scruff of the neck
    and made them give back what they'd stolen.
I thought, 'I'll die peacefully in my own bed,
    grateful for a long and full life,
A life deep-rooted and well-watered,
    a life limber and dew-fresh,
My soul suffused with glory
    and my body robust until the day I die.'

"Men and women listened when I spoke,
    hung expectantly on my every word.
After I spoke, they'd be quiet,

taking it all in.
They welcomed my counsel like spring rain,
    drinking it all in.
When I smiled at them, they could hardly believe it;
    their faces lit up, their troubles took wing!
I was their leader, establishing the mood
    and setting the pace by which they lived.
    Where I led, they followed.

30

The Pain Never Lets Up

"But no longer. Now I'm the butt of their jokes—
    young ruffians! whippersnappers!
Why, I considered their fathers
    mere inexperienced pups.
But they are worse than dogs—good for nothing,
    stray, mangy animals,
Half-starved, scavenging the back alleys,
    howling at the moon;
Homeless guttersnipes
    chewing on old bones and licking old tin cans;
Outcasts from the community,
    cursed as dangerous delinquents.
Nobody would put up with them;
    they were driven from the neighborhood.
You could hear them out there at the edge of town,
    yelping and barking, huddled in junkyards,
A gang of beggars and no-names,
    thrown out on their ears.

"But now I'm the one they're after,
    mistreating me, taunting and mocking.
They abhor me, they abuse me.
    How dare those scoundrels—they spit in my face!
Now that God has undone me and left me in a heap,
    they hold nothing back. Anything goes.
They come at me from my blind side,
    trip me up, then jump on me while I'm down.
They throw every kind of obstacle in my path,
    determined to ruin me—
    and no one lifts a finger to help me!
They violate my broken body,
    trample through the rubble of my ruined life.
Terrors assault me—
    my dignity in shreds,
    salvation up in smoke.

"And now my life drains out,
    as suffering seizes and grips me hard.
Night gnaws at my bones;
    the pain never lets up.
I am tied hand and foot, my neck in a noose.
    I twist and turn.
Thrown facedown in the muck,
    I'm a muddy mess, inside and out.

WHAT DID I DO TO DESERVE THIS?

"I shout for help, God, and get nothing, no answer!
    I stand to face you in protest, and you give me a blank stare!

You've turned into my tormenter—
>	you slap me around, knock me about.
You raised me up so I was riding high
>	and then dropped me, and I crashed.
I know you're determined to kill me,
>	to put me six feet under.

"What did I do to deserve this?
>	Did I ever hit anyone who was calling for help?
Haven't I wept for those who live a hard life,
>	been heartsick over the lot of the poor?
But where did it get me?
>	I expected good but evil showed up.
>	I looked for light but darkness fell.
My stomach's in a constant churning, never settles down.
>	Each day confronts me with more suffering.
I walk under a black cloud. The sun is gone.
>	I stand in the congregation and protest.
I howl with the jackals,
>	I hoot with the owls.
I'm black and blue all over,
>	burning up with fever.
My fiddle plays nothing but the blues;
>	my mouth harp wails laments.

31

WHAT CAN I EXPECT FROM GOD?

"I made a solemn pact with myself
>	never to undress a girl with my eyes.

So what can I expect from God?
    What do I deserve from God Almighty above?
Isn't calamity reserved for the wicked?
    Isn't disaster supposed to strike those who do wrong?
Isn't God looking, observing how I live?
    Doesn't he mark every step I take?

"Have I walked hand in hand with falsehood,
    or hung out in the company of deceit?
Weigh me on a set of honest scales
    so God has proof of my integrity.
If I've strayed off the straight and narrow,
    wanted things I had no right to,
    messed around with sin,
Go ahead, then—
    give my portion to someone who deserves it.

"If I've let myself be seduced by a woman
    and conspired to go to bed with her,
Fine, my wife has every right to go ahead
    and sleep with anyone she wants to.
For disgusting behavior like that,
    I'd deserve the worst punishment you could hand out.
Adultery is a fire that burns the house down;
    I wouldn't expect anything I count dear to survive it.

"Have I ever been unfair to my employees
    when they brought a complaint to me?
What, then, will I do when God confronts me?
    When God examines my books, what can I say?

74

Didn't the same God who made me, make them?
　　Aren't we all made of the same stuff, equals before God?

"Have I ignored the needs of the poor,
　　turned my back on the indigent,
Taken care of my own needs and fed my own face
　　while they languished?
Wasn't my home always open to them?
　　Weren't they always welcome at my table?

"Have I ever left a poor family shivering in the cold
　　when they had no warm clothes?
Didn't the poor bless me when they saw me coming,
　　knowing I'd brought coats from my closet?

"If I've ever used my strength and influence
　　to take advantage of the unfortunate,
Go ahead, break both my arms,
　　cut off all my fingers!
The fear of God has kept me from these things—
　　how else could I ever face him?

IF ONLY SOMEONE WOULD GIVE ME A HEARING!

"Did I set my heart on making big money
　　or worship at the bank?
Did I boast about my wealth,
　　show off because I was well-off?
Was I ever so awed by the sun's brilliance
　　and moved by the moon's beauty

That I let myself become seduced by them
    and worshiped them on the sly?
If so, I would deserve the worst of punishments,
    for I would be betraying God himself.

"Did I ever crow over my enemy's ruin?
    Or gloat over my rival's bad luck?
No, I never said a word of detraction,
    never cursed them, even under my breath.

"Didn't those who worked for me say,
    'He fed us well. There were always second helpings'?
And no stranger ever had to spend a night in the street;
    my doors were always open to travelers.
Did I hide my sin the way Adam did,
    or conceal my guilt behind closed doors
Because I was afraid what people would say,
    fearing the gossip of the neighbors so much
That I turned myself into a recluse?
    You know good and well that I didn't.

"Oh, if only someone would give me a hearing!
    I've signed my name to my defense—let the Almighty One
        answer!
    I want to see my indictment in writing.
Anyone's welcome to read my defense;
    I'll write it on a poster and carry it around town.
I'm prepared to account for every move I've ever made—
    to anyone and everyone, prince or pauper.

"If the very ground that I farm accuses me,
    if even the furrows fill with tears from my abuse,
If I've ever raped the earth for my own profit
    or dispossessed its rightful owners,
Then curse it with thistles instead of wheat,
    curse it with weeds instead of barley."

The words of Job to his three friends were finished.

32   ELIHU SPEAKS

GOD'S SPIRIT MAKES WISDOM POSSIBLE

Job's three friends now fell silent. They were talked out, stymied because Job wouldn't budge an inch—wouldn't admit to an ounce of guilt. Then Elihu lost his temper. (Elihu was the son of Barakel the Buzite from the clan of Ram.) He blazed out in anger against Job for pitting his righteousness against God's. He was also angry with the three friends because they had neither come up with an answer nor proved Job wrong. Elihu had waited with Job while they spoke because they were all older than he. But when he saw that the three other men had exhausted their arguments, he exploded with pent-up anger.

This is what Elihu, son of Barakel the Buzite, said:

"I'm a young man,
    and you are all old and experienced.
That's why I kept quiet
    and held back from joining the discussion.

I kept thinking, 'Experience will tell.
    The longer you live, the wiser you become.'
But I see I was wrong—it's God's Spirit in a person,
    the breath of the Almighty One, that makes wise human
        insight possible.
The experts have no corner on wisdom;
    getting old doesn't guarantee good sense.
So I've decided to speak up. Listen well!
    I'm going to tell you exactly what I think.

"I hung on your words while you spoke,
    listened carefully to your arguments.
While you searched for the right words,
    I was all ears.
And now what have you proved? Nothing.
    Nothing you say has even touched Job.
And don't excuse yourselves by saying, 'We've done our best.
    Now it's up to God to talk sense into him.'
Job has yet to contend with me.
    And rest assured, I won't be using *your* arguments!

"Do you three have nothing else to say?
    Of *course* you don't! You're total frauds!
Why should I wait any longer,
    now that you're stopped dead in your tracks?
I'm ready to speak my piece. That's right!
    It's my turn—and it's about time!
I've got a lot to say,
    and I'm bursting to say it.
The pressure has built up, like lava beneath the earth.

I'm a volcano ready to blow.
I *have* to speak—I have no choice.
    I have to say what's on my heart,
And I'm going to say it straight—
    the truth, the whole truth, and nothing but the truth.
I was never any good at bootlicking;
    my Maker would make short work of me if I started in now!

33

"So please, Job, hear me out,
    honor me by listening to me.
What I'm about to say
    has been carefully thought out.
I have no ulterior motives in this;
    I'm speaking honestly from my heart.
The Spirit of God made me what I am,
    the breath of God Almighty gave me life!

GOD ALWAYS ANSWERS, ONE WAY OR ANOTHER

"And if you think you can prove me wrong, do it.
    Lay out your arguments. Stand up for yourself!
Look, I'm human—no better than you;
    we're both made of the same kind of mud.
So let's work this through together;
    don't let my aggressiveness overwhelm you.

"Here's what you said.
    I heard you say it with my own ears.

You said, 'I'm pure—I've done nothing wrong.
    Believe me, I'm clean—my conscience is clear.
But God keeps picking on me;
    he treats me like I'm his enemy.
He's thrown me in jail;
    he keeps me under constant surveillance.'

"But let me tell you, Job, you're wrong, dead wrong!
    God is far greater than any human.
So how dare you haul him into court,
    and then complain that he won't answer your charges?
God always answers, one way or another,
    even when people don't recognize his presence.

"In a dream, for instance, a vision at night,
    when men and women are deep in sleep,
    fast asleep in their beds—
God opens their ears
    and impresses them with warnings
To turn them back from something bad they're planning,
    from some reckless choice,
And keep them from an early grave,
    from the river of no return.

"Or, God might get their attention through pain,
    by throwing them on a bed of suffering,
So they can't stand the sight of food,
    have no appetite for their favorite treats.
They lose weight, wasting away to nothing,
    reduced to a bag of bones.

They hang on the cliff-edge of death,
    knowing the next breath may be their last.

"But even then an angel could come,
    a champion—there are thousands of them!—
    to take up your cause,
A messenger who would mercifully intervene,
    canceling the death sentence with the words:
    'I've come up with the ransom!'
Before you know it, you're healed,
    the very picture of health!

"Or, you may fall on your knees and pray—to God's delight!
    You'll see God's smile and celebrate,
    finding yourself set right with God.
You'll sing God's praises to everyone you meet,
    testifying, 'I messed up my life—
    and let me tell you, it wasn't worth it.
But God stepped in and saved me from certain death.
    I'm alive again! Once more I see the light!'

"This is the way God works.
    Over and over again
He pulls our souls back from certain destruction
    so we'll see the light—and *live* in the light!

"Keep listening, Job.
    Don't interrupt—I'm not finished yet.
But if you think of anything I should know, tell me.
    There's nothing I'd like better than to see your name
        cleared.

Meanwhile, keep listening. Don't distract me with
        interruptions.
    I'm going to teach you the basics of wisdom."

34   ELIHU'S SECOND SPEECH

IT'S IMPOSSIBLE FOR GOD TO DO EVIL

Elihu continued:

"So, my fine friends—listen to me,
    and see what you think of this.
Isn't it just common sense—
    as common as the sense of taste—
To put our heads together
    and figure out what's going on here?

"We've all heard Job say, 'I'm in the right,
    but God won't give me a fair trial.
When I defend myself, I'm called a liar to my face.
    I've done nothing wrong, and I get punished anyway.'
Have you ever heard anything to beat this?
    Does nothing faze this man Job?
Do you think he's spent too much time in bad company,
    hanging out with the wrong crowd,
So that now he's parroting their line:
    'It doesn't pay to try to please God'?

"You're veterans in dealing with these matters;
    certainly we're of one mind on this.

It's impossible for God to do anything evil;
    no way can the Mighty One do wrong.
He makes us pay for exactly what we've done—no more,
        no less.
    Our chickens always come home to roost.
It's impossible for God to do anything wicked,
    for the Mighty One to subvert justice.
He's the one who runs the earth!
    He cradles the whole world in his hand!
If he decided to hold his breath,
    every man, woman, and child would die for lack of air.

GOD IS WORKING BEHIND THE SCENES

"So, Job, use your head;
    this is all pretty obvious.
Can someone who hates order, keep order?
    Do you dare condemn the righteous, mighty God?
Doesn't God always tell it like it is,
    exposing corrupt rulers as scoundrels and criminals?
Does he play favorites with the rich and famous and slight
        the poor?
    Isn't he equally responsible to everybody?
Don't people who deserve it die without notice?
    Don't wicked rulers tumble to their doom?
When the so-called great ones are wiped out,
    we know God is working behind the scenes.

"He has his eyes on every man and woman.
    He doesn't miss a trick.

There is no night dark enough, no shadow deep enough,
    to hide those who do evil.
God doesn't need to gather any more evidence;
    their sin is an open-and-shut case.
He deposes the so-called high and mighty without asking
        questions,
    and replaces them at once with others.
Nobody gets by with anything; overnight,
    judgment is signed, sealed, and delivered.
He punishes the wicked for their wickedness
    out in the open where everyone can see it,
Because they quit following him,
    no longer even thought about him or his ways.
Their apostasy was announced by the cry of the poor;
    the cry of the afflicted got God's attention.

Because You Refuse to Live on God's Terms

"If God is silent, what's that to you?
    If he turns his face away, what can you do about it?
But whether silent or hidden, he's there, ruling,
    so that those who hate God won't take over
    and ruin people's lives.

"So why don't you simply confess to God?
    Say, 'I sinned, but I'll sin no more.
Teach me to see what I still don't see.
    Whatever evil I've done, I'll do it no more.'
Just because you refuse to live on God's terms,
    do you think he should start living on yours?

You choose. I can't do it for you.
    Tell me what you decide.

"All right-thinking people say—
    and the wise who have listened to me concur—
'Job is an ignoramus.
    He talks utter nonsense.'
Job, you need to be pushed to the wall and called to account
    for wickedly talking back to God the way you have.
You've compounded your original sin
    by rebelling against God's discipline,
Defiantly shaking your fist at God,
    piling up indictments against the Almighty One."

35 ELIHU'S THIRD SPEECH

WHEN GOD MAKES CREATION A CLASSROOM

Elihu lit into Job again:

"Does this kind of thing make any sense?
    First you say, 'I'm perfectly innocent before God.'
And then you say, 'It doesn't make a bit of difference
    whether I've sinned or not.'

"Well, I'm going to show you
    that you don't know what you're talking about,
    neither you nor your friends.
Look up at the sky. Take a long hard look.

See those clouds towering above you?
If you sin, what difference could that make to God?
    No matter how much you sin, will it matter to him?
Even if you're good, what would God get out of that?
    Do you think he's dependent on your accomplishments?
The only ones who care whether you're good or bad
    are your family and friends and neighbors.
    God's not dependent on your behavior.

"When times get bad, people cry out for help.
    They cry for relief from being kicked around,
But never give God a thought when things go well,
    when God puts spontaneous songs in their hearts,
When God sets out the entire creation as a science classroom,
    using birds and beasts to teach wisdom.
People are arrogantly indifferent to God—
    until, of course, they're in trouble,
    and then God is indifferent to them.
There's nothing behind such prayers except panic;
    the Almighty pays them no mind.
So why would he notice you
    just because you say you're tired of waiting to be heard,
Or waiting for him to get good and angry
    and do something about the world's problems?

"Job, you talk sheer nonsense—
    nonstop nonsense!"

36

THOSE WHO LEARN FROM THEIR SUFFERING

Here Elihu took a deep breath, but kept going:

"Stay with me a little longer. I'll convince you.
>   There's still more to be said on God's side.
I learned all this firsthand from the Source;
>   everything I know about justice I owe to my Maker
>   himself.
Trust me, I'm giving you undiluted truth;
>   believe me, I know these things inside and out.

"It's true that God is all-powerful,
>   but he doesn't bully innocent people.
For the wicked, though, it's a different story—
>   he doesn't give them the time of day,
>   but champions the rights of their victims.
He never takes his eyes off the righteous;
>   he honors them lavishly, promotes them endlessly.
When things go badly,
>   when affliction and suffering descend,
God tells them where they've gone wrong,
>   shows them how their pride has caused their trouble.
He forces them to heed his warning,
>   tells them they must repent of their bad life.
If they obey and serve him,
>   they'll have a good, long life on easy street.
But if they disobey, they'll be cut down in their prime
>   and never know the first thing about life.

Angry people without God pile grievance upon grievance,
    always blaming others for their troubles.
Living it up in sexual excesses,
    virility wasted, they die young.
But those who learn from their suffering,
    God delivers from their suffering.

OBSESSED WITH PUTTING THE BLAME ON GOD

"Oh, Job, don't you see how God's wooing you
    from the jaws of danger?
How he's drawing you into wide-open places—
    inviting you to feast at a table laden with blessings?
And here you are laden with the guilt of the wicked,
    obsessed with putting the blame on *God*!
Don't let your great riches mislead you;
    don't think you can bribe your way out of this.
Did you plan to buy your way out of this?
    Not on your life!
And don't think that night,
    when people sleep off their troubles,
    will bring you any relief.
Above all, don't make things worse with more evil—
    that's what's behind your suffering as it is!

"Do you have any idea how powerful God is?
    Have you ever heard of a teacher like him?
Has anyone ever had to tell him what to do,
    or correct him, saying, 'You did that all wrong!'?
Remember, then, to praise his workmanship,

which is so often celebrated in song.
Everybody sees it;
> nobody is too far away to see it.

No One Can Escape From God

"Take a long, hard look. See how great he is—infinite,
> greater than anything you could ever imagine or figure out!

"He pulls water up out of the sea,
> distills it, and fills up his rain-cloud cisterns.
Then the skies open up
> and pour out soaking showers on everyone.
Does anyone have the slightest idea how this happens?
> How he arranges the clouds, how he speaks in thunder?
Just look at that lightning, his sky-filling light show
> illumining the dark depths of the sea!
These are the symbols of his sovereignty,
> his generosity, his loving care.
He hurls arrows of light,
> taking sure and accurate aim.
The High God roars in the thunder,
> angry against evil.

37

"Whenever this happens, my heart stops—
> I'm stunned, I can't catch my breath.
Listen to it! Listen to his thunder,
> the rolling, rumbling thunder of his voice.

89

He lets loose his lightnings from horizon to horizon,
     lighting up the earth from pole to pole.
In their wake, the thunder echoes his voice,
     powerful and majestic.
He lets out all the stops, he holds nothing back.
     No one can mistake that voice—
His word thundering so wondrously,
     his mighty acts staggering our understanding.
He orders the snow, 'Blanket the earth!'
     and the rain, 'Soak the whole countryside!'
No one can escape the weather—it's *there*.
     And no one can escape from God.
Wild animals take shelter,
     crawling into their dens,
When blizzards roar out of the north
     and freezing rain crusts the land.
It's God's breath that forms the ice,
     it's God's breath that turns lakes and rivers solid.
And yes, it's God who fills clouds with rainwater
     and hurls lightning from them every which way.
He puts them through their paces—first this way,
          then that—
     commands them to do what he says all over the world.
Whether for discipline or grace or extravagant love,
     he makes sure they make their mark.

A Terrible Beauty Streams From God

"Job, are you listening? Have you noticed all this?
     Stop in your tracks! Take in God's miracle-wonders!

Do you have any idea how God does it all,
    how he makes bright lightning from dark storms,
How he piles up the cumulus clouds—
    all these miracle-wonders of a perfect Mind?
Why, you don't even know how to keep cool
    on a sweltering hot day,
So how could you even dream
    of making a dent in that hot-tin-roof sky?

"If you're so smart, give us a lesson in how to address God.
    We're in the dark and can't figure it out.
Do you think I'm dumb enough to challenge God?
    Wouldn't that just be asking for trouble?
No one in his right mind stares straight at the sun
    on a clear and cloudless day.
As gold comes from the northern mountains,
    so a terrible beauty streams from God.

"Mighty God! Far beyond our reach!
    Unsurpassable in power and justice!
    It's unthinkable that he'd treat anyone unfairly.
So bow to him in deep reverence, one and all!
    If you're wise, you'll most certainly worship him."

38   GOD CONFRONTS JOB

HAVE YOU GOTTEN TO THE BOTTOM OF THINGS?

And now, finally, GOD answered Job from the eye of a violent
storm. He said:

"Why do you confuse the issue?
     Why do you talk without knowing what you're talking
          about?
Pull yourself together, Job!
     Up on your feet! Stand tall!
I have some questions for you,
     and I want some straight answers.
Where were you when I created the earth?
     Tell me, since you know so much!
Who decided on its size? Certainly you'll know that!
     Who came up with the blueprints and measurements?
How was its foundation poured,
     and who set the cornerstone,
While the morning stars sang in chorus
     and all the angels shouted praise?
And who took charge of the ocean
     when it gushed forth like a baby from the womb?
That was me! I wrapped it in soft clouds,
     and tucked it in safely at night.
Then I made a playpen for it,
     a strong playpen so it couldn't run loose,
And said, 'Stay here, this is your place.
     Your wild tantrums are confined to this place.'

"And have you ever ordered Morning, 'Get up!'
     told Dawn, 'Get to work!'
So you could seize Earth like a blanket
     and shake out the wicked like cockroaches?
As the sun brings everything to light,
     brings out all the colors and shapes,

The cover of darkness is snatched from the wicked—
    they're caught in the very act!

"Have you ever gotten to the true bottom of things,
    explored the labyrinthine caves of deep ocean?
Do you know the first thing about death?
    Do you have one clue regarding death's dark mysteries?
And do you have any idea how large this earth is?
    Speak up if you have even the beginning of an answer.

"Do you know where Light comes from
    and where Darkness lives
So you can take them by the hand
    and lead them home when they get lost?
Why, of *course* you know that.
    You've known them all your life,
    grown up in the same neighborhood with them!

"Have you ever traveled to where snow is made,
    seen the vault where hail is stockpiled,
The arsenals of hail and snow that I keep in readiness
    for times of trouble and battle and war?
Can you find your way to where lightning is launched,
    or to the place from which the wind blows?
Who do you suppose carves canyons
    for the downpours of rain, and charts
    the route of thunderstorms
That bring water to unvisited fields,
    deserts no one ever lays eyes on,
Drenching the useless wastelands
    so they're carpeted with wildflowers and grass?

And who do you think is the father of rain and dew,
    the mother of ice and frost?
You don't for a minute imagine
    these marvels of weather just happen, do you?

"Can you catch the eye of the beautiful Pleiades sisters,
    or distract Orion from his hunt?
Can you get Venus to look your way,
    or get the Great Bear and her cubs to come out and play?
Do you know the first thing about the sky's constellations
    and how they affect things on Earth?

"Can you get the attention of the clouds,
    and commission a shower of rain?
Can you take charge of the lightning bolts
    and have them report to you for orders?

WHAT DO YOU HAVE TO SAY FOR YOURSELF?

"Who do you think gave weather-wisdom to the ibis,
    and storm-savvy to the rooster?
Does anyone know enough to number all the clouds
    or tip over the rain barrels of heaven
When the earth is cracked and dry,
    the ground baked hard as a brick?

"Can you teach the lioness to stalk her prey
    and satisfy the appetite of her cubs
As they crouch in their den,
    waiting hungrily in their cave?

And who sets out food for the ravens
　　when their young cry to God,
　　　　fluttering about because they have no food?

39

"Do you know the month when mountain goats give birth?
　　Have you ever watched a doe bear her fawn?
Do you know how many months she is pregnant?
　　Do you know the season of her delivery,
　　　　when she crouches down and drops her offspring?
Her young ones flourish and are soon on their own;
　　they leave and don't come back.

"Who do you think set the wild donkey free,
　　opened the corral gates and let him go?
I gave him the whole wilderness to roam in,
　　the rolling plains and wide-open places.
He laughs at his city cousins, who are harnessed and harried.
　　He's oblivious to the cries of teamsters.
He grazes freely through the hills,
　　nibbling anything that's green.

"Will the wild buffalo condescend to serve you,
　　volunteer to spend the night in your barn?
Can you imagine hitching your plow to a buffalo
　　and getting him to till your fields?
He's hugely strong, yes, but could you trust him,
　　would you dare turn the job over to him?
You wouldn't for a minute depend on him, would you,
　　to do what you said when you said it?

"The ostrich flaps her wings futilely—
    all those beautiful feathers, but useless!
She lays her eggs on the hard ground,
    leaves them there in the dirt, exposed to the weather,
Not caring that they might get stepped on and cracked
    or trampled by some wild animal.
She's negligent with her young, as if they weren't even hers.
    She cares nothing about anything.
She wasn't created very smart, that's for sure,
    wasn't given her share of good sense.
But when she runs, oh, how she runs,
    laughing, leaving horse and rider in the dust.

"Are you the one who gave the horse his prowess
    and adorned him with a shimmering mane?
Did you create him to prance proudly
    and strike terror with his royal snorts?
He paws the ground fiercely, eager and spirited,
    then charges into the fray.
He laughs at danger, fearless,
    doesn't shy away from the sword.
The banging and clanging
    of quiver and lance don't faze him.
He quivers with excitement, and at the trumpet blast
    races off at a gallop.
At the sound of the trumpet he neighs mightily,
    smelling the excitement of battle from a long way off,
    catching the rolling thunder of the war cries.

"Was it through your knowhow that the hawk learned to fly,
    soaring effortlessly on thermal updrafts?

Did you command the eagle's flight,
and teach her to build her nest in the heights,
Perfectly at home on the high cliff-face,
invulnerable on pinnacle and crag?
From her perch she searches for prey,
spies it at a great distance.
Her young gorge themselves on carrion;
wherever there's a road kill, you'll see her circling."

40

GOD then confronted Job directly:

"Now what do you have to say for yourself?
Are you going to haul me, the Mighty One, into court and
press charges?"

JOB ANSWERS GOD

I'M READY TO SHUT UP AND LISTEN

Job answered:

"I'm speechless, in awe—words fail me.
I should never have opened my mouth!
I've talked too much, way too much.
I'm ready to shut up and listen."

GOD'S SECOND SET OF QUESTIONS

I WANT STRAIGHT ANSWERS

GOD addressed Job next from the eye of the storm, and this is
what he said:

"I have some more questions for you,
    and I want straight answers.

"Do you presume to tell me what I'm doing wrong?
    Are you calling me a sinner so you can be a saint?
Do you have an arm like my arm?
    Can you shout in thunder the way I can?
Go ahead, show your stuff.
    Let's see what you're made of, what you can do.
Unleash your outrage.
    Target the arrogant and lay them flat.
Target the arrogant and bring them to their knees.
        Stop the wicked in their tracks—make mincemeat of
            them!
Dig a mass grave and dump them in it—
    faceless corpses in an unmarked grave.
I'll gladly step aside and hand things over to you—
    you can surely save yourself with no help from me!

"Look at the land beast, Behemoth. I created him
        as well as you.
    Grazing on grass, docile as a cow—
Just look at the strength of his back,
    the powerful muscles of his belly.
His tail sways like a cedar in the wind;
    his huge legs are like beech trees.
His skeleton is made of steel,
    every bone in his body hard as steel.
Most magnificent of all my creatures,
    but I still lead him around like a lamb!

The grass-covered hills serve him meals,
 while field mice frolic in his shadow.
He takes afternoon naps under shade trees,
 cools himself in the reedy swamps,
Lazily cool in the leafy shadows
 as the breeze moves through the willows.
And when the river rages he doesn't budge,
 stolid and unperturbed even when the Jordan goes wild.
But you'd never want him for a pet—
 you'd never be able to housebreak him!

41

I RUN THIS UNIVERSE

"Or can you pull in the sea beast, Leviathan, with a fly rod
 and stuff him in your creel?
Can you lasso him with a rope,
 or snag him with an anchor?
Will he beg you over and over for mercy,
 or flatter you with flowery speech?
Will he apply for a job with you
 to run errands and serve you the rest of your life?
Will you play with him as if he were a pet goldfish?
 Will you make him the mascot of the neighborhood
  children?
Will you put him on display in the market
 and have shoppers haggle over the price?
Could you shoot him full of arrows like a pin cushion,
 or drive harpoons into his huge head?

If you so much as lay a hand on him,
    you won't live to tell the story.
What hope would you have with such a creature?
    Why, one look at him would do you in!
If you can't hold your own against his glowering visage,
    how, then, do you expect to stand up to *me*?
Who could confront me and get by with it?
    I'm in *charge* of all this—I *run* this universe!

"But I've more to say about Leviathan, the sea beast,
    his enormous bulk, his beautiful shape.
Who would even dream of piercing that tough skin
    or putting those jaws into bit and bridle?
And who would dare knock at the door of his mouth
    filled with row upon row of fierce teeth?
His pride is invincible;
    nothing can make a dent in that pride.
Nothing can get through that proud skin—
    impervious to weapons and weather,
The thickest and toughest of hides,
    impenetrable!

"He snorts and the world lights up with fire,
    he blinks and the dawn breaks.
Comets pour out of his mouth,
    fireworks arc and branch.
Smoke erupts from his nostrils
    like steam from a boiling pot.
He blows and fires blaze;
    flames of fire stream from his mouth.

All muscle he is—sheer and seamless muscle.
    To meet him is to dance with death.
Sinewy and lithe,
    there's not a soft spot in his entire body—
As tough inside as out,
    rock-hard, invulnerable.
Even angels run for cover when he surfaces,
    cowering before his tail-thrashing turbulence.
Javelins bounce harmlessly off his hide,
    harpoons ricochet wildly.
Iron bars are so much straw to him,
    bronze weapons beneath notice.
Arrows don't even make him blink;
    bullets make no more impression than raindrops.
A battle axe is nothing but a splinter of kindling;
    he treats a brandished harpoon as a joke.
His belly is armor-plated, inexorable—
    unstoppable as a barge.
He roils deep ocean the way you'd boil water,
    he whips the sea like you'd whip an egg into batter.
With a luminous trail stretching out behind him,
    you might think Ocean had grown a gray beard!
There's nothing on this earth quite like him,
    not an ounce of fear in *that* creature!
He surveys all the high and mighty—
    king of the ocean, king of the deep!"

42   JOB WORSHIPS GOD

I Babbled On About Things Far Beyond Me

Job answered GOD:

"I'm convinced: You can do anything and everything.
    Nothing and no one can upset your plans.
You asked, 'Who is this muddying the water,
    ignorantly confusing the issue, second-guessing my
        purposes?'
I admit it. I was the one. I babbled on about things far
        beyond me,
    made small talk about wonders way over my head.
You told me, 'Listen, and let me do the talking.
    Let me ask the questions. *You* give the answers.'
I admit I once lived by rumors of you;
    now I have it all firsthand—from my own eyes and ears!
I'm sorry—forgive me. I'll never do that again, I promise!
    I'll never again live on crusts of hearsay, crumbs of rumor."

GOD RESTORES JOB

I Will Accept His Prayer

After GOD had finished addressing Job, he turned to Eliphaz the
Temanite and said, "I've had it with you and your two friends.
I'm fed up! You haven't been honest either with me or about me—
not the way my friend Job has. So here's what you must do. Take
seven bulls and seven rams, and go to my friend Job. Sacrifice a
burnt offering on your own behalf. My friend Job will pray for

you, and I will accept his prayer. He will ask me not to treat you as you deserve for talking nonsense about me, and for not being honest with me, as he has."

They did it. Eliphaz the Temanite, Bildad the Shuhite, and Zophar the Naamathite did what GOD commanded. And GOD accepted Job's prayer.

After Job had interceded for his friends, GOD restored his fortune—and then doubled it! All his brothers and sisters and friends came to his house and celebrated. They told him how sorry they were, and consoled him for all the trouble GOD had brought him. Each of them brought generous house-warming gifts.

GOD blessed Job's later life even more than his earlier life. He ended up with fourteen thousand sheep, six thousand camels, one thousand teams of oxen, and one thousand donkeys. He also had seven sons and three daughters. He named the first daughter Dove, the second, Cinnamon, and the third, Darkeyes. There was not a woman in that country as beautiful as Job's daughters. Their father treated them as equals with their brothers, providing the same inheritance.

Job lived on another hundred and forty years, living to see his children and grandchildren—four generations of them! Then he died—an old man, a full life.